Level Four

· gentle ·
GRAMMAR

An Adaptation of New Language Exercises for Primary Schools
by C. C. Long

Copyright © 2018 by Large Family Mothering

All rights reserved.

ISBN-13: 978-1720825821

ISBN-10: 1720825823

Visit: momdelights.com

PREFACE

(Excerpted and adapted from the original book.)

INSTRUCTION in language often deals too much with the forms of sentences and too little with thought. Grammatical drill has little effect upon the correctness of every-day expression. The child should be continually engaged in forming exact ideas about objects of study, and in expressing them clearly and accurately. Language is a medium, merely, for the *expression of thought,* and it is important that its nature and purpose be kept in mind.

The value of the lessons in this book is to be sought in the habits of observation and reflection they teach, and in the practice they give in forming exact ideas, and in expressing them clearly. Things seen every day, pictures, choice stories, animals, letter-writing, etc.,—subjects upon which the thoughts, of children exercise themselves spontaneously,—furnish material for these lessons.

The terms "noun," "verb," "adjective," etc., have been used for convenience, and not for the purpose of definition and minute grammatical classification. The children will soon become familiar with them and will use them properly, just as they use many other class words which they can not define formally.

Most of the exercises in this book have been subjected to the test of class use. It is believed that they will commend themselves to teachers who are seeking rational methods of instruction

Introduction

And Instructions

I have observed that, **if not corrected early-on, some habits of poor grammar and spelling can become like permanent marker on the walls of a young child's mind.** Even though I agree heartily with the idea that children learn spelling and grammar best by reading and writing, my own children have needed more specific instruction. However, I'm not willing to overburden them with a complete English program in every grade. This repetition of the same information year-after-year kills the love of language in children.

I needed to find a program that was:

- Something I could put on "auto pilot"

- Quick (for kids who already had trouble sitting still for reading and math)

- Not technical

- Cheap and easy to put together (not too much printing, cutting, pasting, etc., etc., etc.)

Early-on I discovered *Simply Grammar*, an expanded version of Charlotte Mason's *First Grammar Lessons*. However, the work was meant to be done orally, which was too much work for a woman juggling children at six different levels at the same time.

Finally, I stumbled upon Dollar Homeschool in *The Old Schoolhouse* magazine. This company specializes in collecting school books from times past and making them available in digital

form for modern use. These materials were written before the Progressive education movement in America, a time before humanism and its psychobabble began to rule the way children were taught.

Included on one of the CD's from Dollar Homeschool was a collection of grammar books, and in particular two which I found very interesting. These were written by a person by the name of C. C. Long and were entitled *New Language Exercises for Primary Schools* part one and part two (I like to refer to them as "Long's Language"). **As I read through them I became more and more excited; this was finally the answer, the tool that would help fill the gap and turn my beginning readers into confident, competent writers!**

For one thing, the first lessons are not about nouns and verbs. There is actually very little mentioned in the first book about grammar at all, although grammar is the subject. Instead, children are asked to write about themselves, where they live, etc. The lessons present sentences as "statements" including a subject and a predicate without ever mentioning the technical terms. Within the first 50 lessons, my little ones have been able to write short paragraphs that describe familiar objects such as a ball, a cow, etc.

For another thing, the lessons are oh, so short! The instructions are usually one or two sentences long, and the exercise is not more than six to twelve short sentences (that follow a formula, so there is not that much thinking involved). If a child is focused, which is easy to do because of the simplicity, the longest lesson takes less than 15 minutes to complete!

Besides all this, the work is mostly self-directed. The learning is gradual, no great leaps are expected from one day to another, so little instruction or oversight is necessary. This is certainly a win/win for us moms of many! My children come away from the lessons feeling accomplished and energized without feeling frustrated. Before I realize it they are well on their way to being successful writers!

After I published a post on my blog recommending this resource, I realized there was a way to make things even easier (both for me and for my readers).

So, I finally sat down with some computer software and began the process of taking the original book and re-engineering it for modern use.

The result is what you see here. As an answer to prayer, I was able to come up with a way that streamlined the lessons and created a work text of sorts, with the original directions and copywork presented with places directly adjoining for the child to complete the work. **The instructions are included in each page – no extra searching,** no lugging around a teacher's manual, no loss due to distraction between the printed page and the actual work.

While I tried to keep to the flavor of the original work, I did tweak the lessons in a few areas, including some correction where the wording was a bit too archaic. I also restructured some of the composition lessons and even wrote a few to add that were more appropriate where necessary.

You will probably want to spend a minute or two on each lesson just to make sure the instructions are understood, and I would also check up to make sure they are done with neatness (remember, a little done well is better than a lot done poorly).

Easy as pie, right?

Please note: You won't want your child to attempt this level until he/she has a good understanding of the different types of sentences and has a basic grasp of punctuation. The best preparation for this fourth level is the first, second and third levels of *Gentle Grammar*.

Blessings,

Sherry

P.S. For any further information on this or any other of our projects, please visit our site, momdelights.com

LANGUAGE EXERCISES
FOURTH READER GRADE

FORMS OF NOUNS

Lesson 1. — Nouns usually have four forms, two for the singular, such as *boy, boy's;* two for the plural, as *boys, boys'*.

Fill in with the different forms of these nouns:

child	Child's	Children	Children's
man			
woman			
pony			
calf			
goose			
fly			
fox			
baby			
thief			
knife			
mouse			
lady			

LANGUAGE EXERCISES
FOURTH READER GRADE

FORMS OF NOUNS

Lesson 2. — *Change these sentences so that each shall contain a word in the possessive form.*

EX.	The coat *of the boy* is soiled.
	The *boy's coat* is soiled.
1.	The wing *of the eagle* is strong.
2.	The mane *of the lion* is shaggy.
3.	The foot *of the horse* is tender.
4.	The teeth *of the dog* are sharp and strong.
5.	The eyes *of the children* are very bright.
6.	The names *of the men* have been erased.
7.	Are the wings *of the butterflies* pretty?

LANGUAGE EXERCISES
FOURTH READER GRADE

Lesson 3. — *Dictation. Make sure and study carefully and go over every part thoroughly before the dictation. Write on the following page.*

I.

Abraham Lincoln's education was simple. He read few books, but mastered all he read. Bunyan's *Pilgrim's Progress, Aesop's Fables,* and the *Life of Washington* were his favorites.

II.

Henry Wadsworth Longfellow, the distinguished American poet, was born in Portland, Maine, Feb. 27, 1807. He died March 24, 1882.

TO THE TEACHER: Read each sentence slowly. Do not repeat. These pages can be found on the last pages.

LANGUAGE EXERCISES
FOURTH READER GRADE

Lesson 3. — (continued)

I.

II.

LANGUAGE EXERCISES
FOURTH READER GRADE

WORDS USED INSTEAD OF NOUNS.

Lesson 4. — *Copy these statements.*

1. He and I study.

2. You and I play.

3. She and I read.

4. You and she sing.

5. You, Alma, and I came early.

You should say, "He and I," and, "she and I," not, "me and him," or "me and her."

LANGUAGE EXERCISES
FOURTH READER GRADE

WORDS USED INSTEAD OF NOUNS.

Lesson 5. — *Copy these statements. They show the correct use of me, him, her, us, and them.*

1. Charles called me.

2. He called him and me.

3. He called Clarence and me.

4. She came with me.

5. She came with Ella and me.

6. Clara spoke to Fred and me.

7. You asked Maud and me to come.

8. She walked with Mr. Jones and me.

LANGUAGE EXERCISES
FOURTH READER GRADE

	WORDS THAT DESCRIBE, OR ADJECTIVES.
	Lesson 6. — *Use each of these words to describe some object as to* form *or* size; as,
	The hoop is round. Some windows are square.
1.	long
2.	short
3.	wide
4.	broad
5.	narrow
6.	thin
7.	thick
8.	slender

LANGUAGE EXERCISES
FOURTH READER GRADE

	WORDS THAT DESCRIBE, OR ADJECTIVES.
	Lesson 6. — (continued)
9.	high
10.	tall
11.	big
12.	little
13.	wee
14.	deep
15.	shallow
16.	flat
17.	heavy

LANGUAGE EXERCISES
FOURTH READER GRADE

WORDS USED INSTEAD OF NOUNS.

Lesson 7. — *Use these words in describing boys and girls that you know.*

Example: A kind boy. A manly boy. A thoughtful boy.

My companion is a kind, manly, thoughtful boy.

1. rude, cruel, sullen

2. kind, manly brave

3. pale, slender, polite

4. polite, honest, agreeable

LANGUAGE EXERCISES
FOURTH READER GRADE

WORDS USED INSTEAD OF NOUNS.

Lesson 7. — (continued)

5. delicate, thoughtful, lady-like

6. Thoughtless, careless, slender

Doodle Space:

LANGUAGE EXERCISES
FOURTH READER GRADE

WORDS USED INSTEAD OF NOUNS.

Lesson 8. — Which of the following words might describe a song? A fire? A river? A path? A day? The sky? Ice?

Example: A smooth river. A clear river. A winding river.

A smooth, clear, and winding river wound its way through the valley.

wet	clear	bright	fleecy
cold	large	stormy	gloomy
hard	warm	dreary	winding
blue	white	narrow	graveled
long	sweet	smooth	transparent

1. a song

2. a river

LANGUAGE EXERCISES
FOURTH READER GRADE

	Lesson 8. — (continued)
3.	a path
4.	a day
5.	the sky
6.	ice

LANGUAGE EXERCISES
FOURTH READER GRADE

Lesson 9. — *Think of a tree you have seen, and describe it orally.*

Where is it? Is it an oak, elm, beech, birch? Is it large, tall, high, small, low? Is the bark smooth or rough? In winter bare or barren? In spring, beautiful foliage (branches, leaves)?

Complete these sentences:

1. The woodman's _____ shall _____ it down.

2. It _____ been my shelter _____ sunshine _____ storm.

3. _____ protect _____ now _____ those _____ would injure or destroy it.

Doodle Space:

LANGUAGE EXERCISES
FOURTH READER GRADE

Lesson 10. — *Write sentences containing the following words.*

Example:
ohn is a large boy.
Henry is larger than John.
Charles is the largest boy in the class.

1. large

2. larger

3. largest

4. big

5. bigger

6. biggest

7. long

LANGUAGE EXERCISES
FOURTH READER GRADE

	Lesson 10. — (continued)
8.	longer
9.	longest
10.	small
11.	smaller
12.	smallest
13.	light
14.	lighter
15.	Lightest
16.	young

LANGUAGE EXERCISES
FOURTH READER GRADE

	Lesson 10. — (continued)
17.	younger
18.	youngest
19.	heavy
20.	heavier
21.	heaviest

LANGUAGE EXERCISES
FOURTH READER GRADE

Lesson 11. — *Fill the blanks as indicated. Write a sentence containing one of the words in the line.*

beautiful	_____ beautiful	_____ beautiful
truthful	_____ truthful	_____ truthful
studious	_____ studious	_____ studious
faithful	_____ faithful	_____ faithful
obedient	_____ obedient	_____ obedient
generous	_____ generous	_____ generous

LANGUAGE EXERCISES
FOURTH READER GRADE

	Lesson 12. — *Write sentences to show that you can use the following words correctly.*
1.	good
2.	better
3.	best
4.	little
5.	less
6.	least
7	bad
8.	worse
9.	worst

LANGUAGE EXERCISES
FOURTH READER GRADE

	Lesson 12. — (continued)
10.	far
11.	farther
12.	farthest
	Doodle space:

LANGUAGE EXERCISES
FOURTH READER GRADE

Lesson 13. — *Fill blanks in these sentences.*

1. The people of England speak the _____ language.

2. The _____ language is spoken in Holland.

3. In Spain they read the _____ language.

4. In France the people write the _____ language.

5. A party of Swedes sang _____ songs.

6. The _____ people live in Scotland.

7. The _____ language is spoken in Italy.

We should guard against the inappropriate and extravagant use of descriptive terms.

"Just too lovely for anything," to express what is simply pleasing; "as tired as I can be," for ordinary fatigue, and similar exaggerations should be avoided.

LANGUAGE EXERCISES
FOURTH READER GRADE

WORDS THAT EXPRESS ACTION, OR VERBS

Lesson 14. — Much care is necessary to avoid error in the use of the following words.

Three forms of each word are given. Be careful in conversation and in writing, that you use *have*, *has*, or *had* only with the third form.

begin	began	begun	ring	rang	rung
choose	chose	chosen	rise	rose	risen
do	did	done	teach	taught	taught
draw	drew	drawn	wear	wore	worn
freeze	froze	frozen	wring	wrung	wrung

Think of a game and give a sentence about it, using the first form, *choose*; the second form; the third form.

1.

2.

3.

Think of an exercise in school and give a sentence about it, using the first form, *draw*; the second form; the third form.

1.

2.

3.

LANGUAGE EXERCISES
FOURTH READER GRADE

Lesson 14. — (continued)

Make sentences about your kite, using the three forms of *rise*.

1.
2.
3.

Make sentences, using the three forms of *do*.

1.
2.
3.

Make sentences using the three forms of *freeze*.

1.
2.
3.

Make sentences using the three forms of *teach*.

1.
2.
3.

LANGUAGE EXERCISES
FOURTH READER GRADE

Lesson 15.

Errors are frequent in the use of *lie* and *lay*. *Lay* is often used for *lie*, and *lie* is sometimes used for *lay*.

To *lie* means to place one's self in a horizontal position; as,

Lie on the lounge, James.

He lay there an hour.

The cat lies by the fire.

It has lain there all day.

The cows are lying in the shade.

They have lain there since morning.

To lay means to put or place (something); as,

Lay the slate on the desk.

He laid the slate on the desk.

The bird has laid five eggs.

She had laid three eggs last week.

The masons lay the brick with care.

They laid the new walk yesterday.

After careful study of the following words, write sentences showing their correct use.

1.	lie
2.	lying

LANGUAGE EXERCISES
FOURTH READER GRADE

	Lesson 15. — (continued)
3.	lay
4.	laying
5.	lay
6.	lain
7.	laid
	Doodle space:

LANGUAGE EXERCISES
FOURTH READER GRADE

WORDS THAT SHOW HOW, OR ADVERBS

Lesson 16. — Birds fly *swiftly*. The horse walks *fast*.

Q. Which word tells what birds do?

A. The word *fly*.

Q. Which word tells *how* they fly?

A. The word *swiftly*.

Q. What does the horse do?

A. The horse *walks*.

Q. Which word tells *how* he walks?

A. The word *fast*.

LANGUAGE EXERCISES
FOURTH READER GRADE

Lesson 17.

| neatly | kindly | gently | pleasantly |
| angrily | wisely | noisily | honestly |

Use one of the above words to tell:

1. How your friend dresses.

2. How the angry driver spoke.

3. How the boy spoke to his sister.

4. How the father advised his son.

5. How the mother lifted her sick child.

6. How the rough boy packed his books.

7. How the teacher addresses her pupils.

8. How the merchant deals with his customers.

LANGUAGE EXERCISES
FOURTH READER GRADE

Lesson 17. — (continued)

Tell how something took place:

1. In the school room.

2. In a game of ball.

3. In painting a house.

4. In walking along on a dark night.

Doodle space:

LANGUAGE EXERCISES
FOURTH READER GRADE

Lesson 18. — *Dictation*

"Why do you grow by the roadside, dear?
    It is all dust and sand;
Come to the violet's shady nook,
    Or join the My-flower's band."

But the daisy said: "The violet's place
    Is better for her, you see;
And the May-flower's place is better for her;
    And mine is the best for me."

Cover up the top and copy here:

LANGUAGE EXERCISES
FOURTH READER GRADE

WORDS THAT SHOW WHEN, OR ADVERBS

Lesson 19. — John studies *now*. Clara came *early*.

Q. What does John do?

A. John *studies*.

Q. What does the word "now" tell?

A. "Now" tells *when* he studies.

Q. What did Clara do?

A. Clara *came*.

Q. What does the word "early" tell?

A. "Early" tells *when* she came.

Write sentences containing these words.

1.	soon
2.	last night
3.	next week
4.	today
5.	after school

LANGUAGE EXERCISES
FOURTH READER GRADE

	Lesson 19. — (continued)
6.	at midnight
7.	yesterday
8.	in the morning
9.	at three o'clock
10.	tomorrow
11.	in the evening
12.	a few weeks ago

LANGUAGE EXERCISES
FOURTH READER GRADE

WORDS THAT SHOW WHERE, OR ADVERBS.

Lesson 20. — Charles sits *here*. Mary stands *there*.

The words *here* and *there* tell *where* actions are done.

Write sentences containing these words.

1. here

2. on the table

3. in the field

4. there

5. in my hand

6. three miles away

7. upstairs

8. in the attic

LANGUAGE EXERCISES
FOURTH READER GRADE

	Lesson 20. — (continued)
9.	over our heads
10.	downstairs
11.	into the water
12.	against the wall

LANGUAGE EXERCISES
FOURTH READER GRADE

ENLARGING SENTENCES.

Lesson 21. — We may enlarge the sentence "The bird flies" by adding a word or phrase to the word "bird"; thus, The *wild* bird flies. The bird *with the long wings* flies.

Enlarge the following sentences by filling each blank with a suitable word or phrase.

1. The _____ man lives in a cottage.
2. The _____ fish were caught in a net.
3. The _____ boy was severely punished.
4. Does the _____ light hurt your eyes?
5. The tree _____ has been blown down.
6. Are the leaves _____ withering?
7. The bell _____ rings loudly.
8. The carpet _____ has bright colors.
9. A boy _____ always tells the truth.

LANGUAGE EXERCISES
FOURTH READER GRADE

ENLARGING SENTENCES.

Lesson 22. — We may further enlarge the sentence by adding a word or phrase to the word "flies"; thus, The bird flies *swiftly*. The bird flies *in the air*.

Enlarge each sentence by filling each blank with a suitable word or phrase.

1. The dog barks _____.

2. The wind blows _____.

3. The fire burns _____.

4. Did the mothers speak _____?

5. Do the clouds move _____?

6. The lambs play _____.

LANGUAGE EXERCISES
FOURTH READER GRADE

ENLARGING SENTENCES.

Lesson 23.

1. *The children sat:* how? where? when?

   In the evening the children sat quietly on the doorstep.

2. *A clock stopped:* what kind? how? when?

   An old clock stopped suddenly one summer morning.

3. *I can hear:* what? when? from where?

   All night long I can hear the noise from my window.

By changing the parts we have the following sentences:

1. The children, in the evening, sat quietly on the doorstep.
2. One summer morning, an old clock stopped suddenly.
3. I can hear, all night long, the noise from my window.

LANGUAGE EXERCISES
FOURTH READER GRADE

ENLARGING SENTENCES.

Lesson 24. — *Enlarge each sentence in this exercise by adding words and phrases.*

1. The fishes swim: how? when? where?

2. The boys play: what? when? where?

3. The snow falls: what kind? how? from where?

4. The children study: what? how? when? where?

5. We shot some birds: what kind? when? where?

LANGUAGE EXERCISES
FOURTH READER GRADE

	Lesson 24. — (continued)
6.	The wind whistles: in what season? what kind of wind? how? through what?
7.	Bees gather: what? when? from what? for what?

LANGUAGE EXERCISES
FOURTH READER GRADE

WHO OR WHICH.

Lesson 25. — I see the man who sings. He fed the horse which was hungry. She mailed the letter which I wrote.

How is *who* used? How is *which* used?

Fill in the blanks:

We use _____ for persons, and _____ for animals or things.

Write three statements showing that you know how to sue the word "who" correctly.

1.
2.
3.

Write three statements showing that you know how to use "which" correctly.

1.
2.
3.

How can you tell when to use "who," and when to use "which"?

LANGUAGE EXERCISES
FOURTH READER GRADE

WHO OR WHOM.

Lesson 26. — *Copy the following sentences, filling the blanks with the word "whom."*

1. Of _____ did you speak?
2. To _____ did you send the book?
3. With _____ were you singing last evening?
4. From _____ did you receive the present?
5. _____ did you see at the church?

Write questions for the following answers.

1. I went with Mary. (With whom did you go?)

2. I spoke to Jane and Ann.

3. We saw her brother Harry.

4. He was speaking of Mr. Jones.

5. I received a present from my father.

LANGUAGE EXERCISES
FOURTH READER GRADE

WHO OR WHOM

Lesson 27. — *Combine each of the following sets of statements into one sentence, like this:*

I saw a man.

The man was sitting on the platform.

I saw a man who was sitting on the platform.

1. I saw a honey bee.

   The honey bee was in the garden.

2. Tea is the dried leaf of a shrub.

   Tea is from China.

3. Cotton is a soft, white substance.

   Cotton grows in the seed-pod of a plant.

LANGUAGE EXERCISES
FOURTH READER GRADE

	Lesson 27. — (continued)
4.	Cotton is gathered from the pod.
	Cotton is cleaned out from the seed.
5.	Wool comes from the fleece of sheep.
	It is shaved from the animal in summer.
6.	Wool is cleaned.
	Wool is sent to the spinner.
7.	Cloth is made of wool.
	Wool is used for outer clothing.

LANGUAGE EXERCISES
FOURTH READER GRADE

Lesson 28. — *Words of similar sound are called "homophones." Write sentences containing the following words:*

1.	beat	
2.	beet	
3.	berry	
4.	bury	
5.	bough	
6.	bow	
7.	break	
8.	brake	

LANGUAGE EXERCISES
FOURTH READER GRADE

	Lesson 28. — (continued)	
9.	capital	
10.	capitol	
11.	cellar	
12.	seller	
13.	coarse	
14.	course	
15.	grate	
16.	great	

LANGUAGE EXERCISES
FOURTH READER GRADE

	Lesson 28. — (continued)	
17.	heal	
18.	heel	
19.	heard	
20.	herd	
21.	knot	
22.	not	
23.	medal	
24.	meddle	

LANGUAGE EXERCISES
FOURTH READER GRADE

	Lesson 28. — (continued)	
25.	pain	
26.	pane	
27.	principal	
28.	principle	
29.	rain	
30.	reign	
	Doodle space:	

LANGUAGE EXERCISES
FOURTH READER GRADE

Lesson 29.. — *Dictation, read from this page, write on the next pages.*

I. Where are you? Here I am. Whose ring is this? It is Mr. Walton's. There are two lead pencils here. One of their points is broken off. Whose are they? The teacher's, I think.

II. "Oh, look!" said John, "whose knife is this?" At whose store does your father buy his groceries? At Mr. Smith's, I think.

Which sounds better, "No, sir, I can't," or, "Yes, ma'am, I'll try?"

III. In some countries the little spotted beetle called "ladybird" is supposed to be a sign of good luck and to indicate fair weather. In Germany the children throw this beetle into the air and exclaim:

Ladybird, ladybird, fly away home;

Bring me good weather whenever you come."

TO THE TEACHER: Read each sentence slowly. Do not repeat. These pages can be found on the last pages.

LANGUAGE EXERCISES
FOURTH READER GRADE

	Lesson 29. — (continued)
I.	
II.	

LANGUAGE EXERCISES
FOURTH READER GRADE

	Lesson 29. — (continued)
III.	

LANGUAGE EXERCISES
FOURTH READER GRADE

STORIES FOR REPRODUCTION

Lesson 31. — *Read the story and reproduce it in your own words.*

1. An old man entered a railroad car and was looking around for a seat. A boy ten or twelve years of age rose up and said, "Take my seat, sir."

   The offer was accepted, and the infirm old man sat down. "Why did you give me your seat?" he inquired of the boy. "Because you are old, sir, and I am a boy!" was the reply.

   Such thoughtfulness for others by young people is a most winning trait of character.

LANGUAGE EXERCISES
FOURTH READER GRADE

STORIES FOR REPRODUCTION

Lesson 31. — *(continued)*

2. There was once a horse that used to pull around a sweep which lifted dirt from the depths of the earth. He was kept at the business for nearly twenty years, until he became too old for further use. So he was turned into a pasture and left to crop the grass without any one to disturb or bother him.

Every morning, after grazing a while, he would start on a tramp, going round and round in a circle, just as he had done for so many years. He would keep it up for hours, and people often stopped to look and wonder what made the old horse walk around in such a solemn way when there was no need of it. It was the force of habit.

The boy or girl who forms bad or good habits in his youth will be led by them when he becomes old, and will be miserable or happy accordingly.

LANGUAGE EXERCISES
FOURTH READER GRADE

Lesson 32. — *Write a description of this picture using the words and phrases provided.*

a small, black horse   saddle

a black mane   stirrups

a long and flowing tail   not to go so fast at first

LANGUAGE EXERCISES
FOURTH READER GRADE

Lesson 33. — *Spring*

Walter went to the country in spring. This a list of what he saw:

1. Birds building nests
2. Young lambs
3. Buds and flowers
4. Mild and pleasant weather
5. Farmers plowing, sowing, planting
6. Fruit trees in bloom

Use the above list to write a paragraph:

LANGUAGE EXERCISES
FOURTH READER GRADE

Lesson 34. — *Summer*

Rachel went to the country in summer. This is a list of what she saw:

1.	Warm weather
2.	Dusty roads
3.	Mowed hay
4.	Cut wheat
5.	Tall corn
6.	Fruit trees filled with fruit

Use the above list to write a paragraph:

LANGUAGE EXERCISES
FOURTH READER GRADE

Lesson 35. — *Autumn*

Louise went to the country in autumn. This is a list of what she saw:

1. Warm days, cool nights
2. Leaves are red and brown
3. Walnuts and apples are gathered
4. Ears of corn are plucked
5. The pumpkins are picked

Use the above list to write a paragraph:

LANGUAGE EXERCISES
FOURTH READER GRADE

Lesson 36. — *Winter*

Frank went to the country in winter. This is a list of what he saw:

1.	Cold
2.	Snow
3.	Few birds
4.	No flowers
5.	Wind whistles
6.	Boys and girls near the fire studying

Use the above list to write a paragraph:

LANGUAGE EXERCISES
FOURTH READER GRADE

Lesson 37. — *Summer and Winter.*

Write carefully what you know about summer and winter, referring to this list:

Summer	Winter
warm	cold
rain, dew	snow, ice
flowers bloom, trees green	flowers dead, trees bare
fruits grow and ripen	fruits no longer weigh down branches
birds sing	pretty singing birds gone

LANGUAGE EXERCISES
FOURTH READER GRADE

Lesson 38. — *life on a Farm.*

Write a composition using the following list:

farmers busy	plowing corn
raking hay	farmer's wife among the milk pans, bright as silver
children free from school, playing in garden	church bells
neighbors gather	talk about the corn
ripening grain	drought
autumn	husking corn
gathering fruit	cold evenings
around the fire	tending to animals in the cold

LANGUAGE EXERCISES
FOURTH READER GRADE

Lesson 39. — *Write a letter to your friend. Tell about something you own that you enjoy, such as a pet or a toy. Invite your friend to come see it.*

Example:

March 15, 2018

Dear Francine,

I hope you are having fun this summer.

We are all having fun because we have a new puppy. It is an Irish Setter named Shadow. We gave him that name because he looks like a miniature of our other dog, Rover.

He is so soft and nice to pet. He sometimes bites, but we are teaching him not to do that. He doesn't bark much, but he does whine when he misses us.

I hope you can come over soon so that you can play with him.

Your friend,

Jeanine

LANGUAGE EXERCISES
FOURTH READER GRADE

Lesson 40. — *Write a letter to your friend. Tell about something you own that you enjoy, such as a pet or a toy. Invite your friend to come see it.*

Example:

March 15, 2018

Dear Francine,

I hope you are having fun this summer.

We are all having fun because we have a new puppy. It is an Irish Setter named Shadow. We gave him that name because he looks like a miniature of our other dog, Rover.

He is so soft and nice to pet. He sometimes bites, but we are teaching him not to do that. He doesn't bark much, but he does whine when he misses us.

I hope you can come over soon so that you can play with him.

Your friend,

Jeanine

LANGUAGE EXERCISES
FOURTH READER GRADE

LANGUAGE EXERCISES
FOURTH READER GRADE

	DICTATIONS
	The dictation exercises are offered separately here to make it easier for you to use them with your child.
	Lesson 3
I.	Abraham Lincoln's education was simple. He read few books, but mastered all he read. Bunyan's *Pilgrim's Progress, Aesop's Fables,* and the *Life of Washington* were his favorites.
II.	Henry Wadsworth Longfellow, the distinguished American poet, was born in Portland, Maine, Feb. 27, 1807. He died March 24, 1882.
	Lesson 18

	"Why do you grow by the roadside, dear?
	    It is all dust and sand;
	Come to the violet's shady nook,
	    Or join the My-flower's band."
	
	But the daisy said: "The violet's place
	    Is better for her, you see;
	And the May-flower's place is better for her;
	    And mine is the best for me."

LANGUAGE EXERCISES
FOURTH READER GRADE

DICTATION EXERCISES FOR PARENTS TO READ ALOUD

Dictation lesson 29.

I. Where are you? Here I am. Whose ring is this? It is Mr. Walton's. There are two lead pencils here. One of their points is broken off. Whose are they? The teacher's, I think.

II. "Oh, look!" said John, "whose knife is this?" At whose store does your father buy his groceries? At Mr. Smith's, I think.

Which sounds better, "No, sir, I can't," or, "Yes, ma'am, I'll try?"

III. In some countries the little spotted beetle called "ladybird" is supposed to be a sign of good luck and to indicate fair weather. In Germany the children throw this beetle into the air and exclaim:

Ladybird, ladybird, fly away home;

Bring me good weather whenever you come."

LANGUAGE EXERCISES
FOURTH READER GRADE

Made in the USA
Middletown, DE
12 May 2023

30484531R00040